Monika Beisner's
# BOOK OF RIDDLES

*Books by Monika Beisner*

AN ADDRESS BOOK

A FOLDING ALPHABET BOOK

MONIKA BEISNER'S BOOK OF RIDDLES

SECRET SPELLS AND CURIOUS CHARMS

*With Alison Lurie*

THE HEAVENLY ZOO

FABULOUS BEASTS

# Monika Beisner's
# BOOK OF RIDDLES

A SUNBURST BOOK

FARRAR, STRAUS AND GIROUX

# For Johannes

Illustrations copyright © 1983 by Monika Beisner
Text of riddles 2, 8, 9, 14, 18, 19, 25, 27, 49, 50, 54, 56, 57, 59, 62,
63, 66, 69, 74, 78, 85, 87, 90, 92, 95 copyright © 1983 by Jonathan Cape Ltd.
All rights reserved
Library of Congress catalog card number: 83-81529
Printed in Singapore
First American edition, 1983
Sunburst edition, 1987

When first I appear I seem mysterious,
But when I am explained I am nothing serious.

## 1

What is it?
It stands on one leg
With its heart in its head.

## 2

My tail is long, my coat is brown,
I like the country, I like the town.
I can live in a house or live in a
shed,
And I come out to play when you
are in bed.

## 3

What is it:
Has a mouth and does not speak,
Has a bed and does not sleep?

## 4

I sleep by day,
I fly by night.
I have no feathers
To aid my flight.

## 5

It has four legs and a foot
And can't walk.
It has a head
And can't talk.

## 6

My face is pale, and full and fair;
And round it beauty spots there are;
By day, indeed, I seem less bright,
I'm only seen sometimes at night.
And when the sun has gone to bed
I then begin to show my head.

## 7

Flip flop fleezy, .
When it is in, it is easy.
But when it is out,
It flops all about.
Flip flop fleezy.

## 8

I prefer a bed of lettuce to any other
kind,
And frolicking about is most often
on my mind.
My ears are long, and short my tail.
If you try to catch me you will fail.

## 9

My first is in ocean but never in sea,
My second's in wasp but never in
bee,
My third is in glider and also in
flight,
My whole is a creature that comes
out at night.

## 10

What force and strength cannot get
through,
I, with a gentle touch, can do;
And many in the street would stand,
Were I not, as a friend, at hand.

## 11

My first is in chocolate but not in
ham,
My second's in cake and also in jam,
My third at tea-time is easily found,
My whole is a friend who's often
around.
What am I?

## 12

I saw a man in white,
He looked quite a sight.
He was not old,
But he stood in the cold.
And when he felt the sun
He started to run.
Who could he be?
Do answer me.

## 13

What lives in winter,
Dies in summer,
And grows with its root upwards?

## 14

My first is in window but not in
pane,
My second's in road but not in lane,
My third is in oval but not in
round,
My fourth is in hearing but not in
sound,
My whole is known as a sign of
peace,
And from Noah's Ark won quick
release.

## 15

What has:
Six legs, two heads,
Four ears, two hands,
But walks
On four feet?

## 16

There dwell four sisters near this
town,
In looks alike, and like in gown.
Round and round in a ring they run,
Chasing each other just for fun.
But even though they gather pace,
Between them there is equal space.

## 17

No head has he but he wears a hat.
No feet has he but he stands up
straight.
On him perhaps a fairy sat,
Weaving a spell one evening late.

## 18

I love to dance
And twist and prance,
I shake my tail,
As away I sail,
Wingless I fly
Into the sky.
What am I?

## 19

My first is in football but isn't in
shoot,
My second's in treasure but isn't in
loot,
My fourth is in swallow and so is my
third,
My whole on a Sunday is far and
wide heard.

## 20

Iron roof
Glass walls
Burns and burns
And never falls.

## 21

Its belly is linen
Its neck velvet
Its mouth music
Its tail a fork.

## 22

My second is performed by my first;
And, it is thought,
A thief by the marks of my whole
Might be caught.

## 23

Four stiff-standers,
Four dillydanders,
Two hookers,
Two lookers,
And a flip-flap.

## 24

Two brothers we are, great burden
we bear
By which we are bitterly pressed;
In truth we may say, we are full all
the day,
But empty when we go to rest.

## 25

My teeth are sharp,
My back is straight,
To cut things up it is my fate.
What am I?

## 26

In marble walls as white as milk
Lined with a skin as soft as silk;
Within a fountain crystal clear
A golden apple does appear.
No doors there are to this
stronghold –
Yet thieves break in and steal the
gold.

## 27

Riddle me ree,
They grow on a tree,
Are smooth, red and shiny,
Not large but quite tiny.
Their hearts are of stone
When they are full grown.

## 28

As I was walking by Padston bay
Upon a cloudy summer's day,
I saw an object smooth and round
Which very sweet and fresh I found.
But as the outside was quite dry
No further use for it had I,
So I threw its skin away.

## 29

First I am as white as snow,
Then as green as grass I grow,
Next I am as red as blood,
Lastly I'm as black as mud.

## 30

There was a little green house;
And in the little green house
There was a little brown house;
And in the little brown house
There was a little yellow house;
And in the little yellow house
There was a little white house;
And in the little white house
There was a little white heart.

## 31

Brown are their toes,
Striped are their clothes,
Tell me this riddle
And you can pull my nose.

## 32

Old Mister Puddididdle
Played in the muddy puddle;
He had yellow socks and shoes
And a cap of greens and blues,
He was often in a muddle.
Now guess the riddle.

## 33

My first is a woman,
My second a bird,
My whole is an insect
I give you my word.

## 34

When she has a root
She has no leaves;
And when she pulls up her root,
The leaves appear.

## 35

Eight were standing
Two were cracking
Two were looking.

## 36

The greater it is
The less you see of it.

## 37

At night they come without being
fetched,
And by day they are lost without
being stolen.

## 38

Come up and let us go;
Go down and here we stay.

## 39

Long legs
Short thighs
Bald head
And bullet eyes.

## 40

I run smoother than any rhyme,
I love to fall but cannot climb.
I tremble at each breath of air,
And yet can heaviest burdens bear.

## 41

Who is he that runs without a leg
With his house on his back?

## 42

Me riddle, me racket,
Suppose I tell you this riddle,
And perhaps not;
There is something moves all day
And all night and never stops.

## 43

I come out of the earth,
I am sold in the market.
He who buys me cuts my tail,
Takes off my suit of silk,
And weeps beside me when I am
dead.

## 44

What has teeth
And can't bite?

## 45

My first is twice in apple
But not once in tart.
My second is in liver
But not in heart.
My third is in giant
And also in ghost.
Whole I'm best when I am roast.

## 46

Four fingers and a thumb,
Yet flesh and blood I have none.

## 47

Long pole, bushy tail.
What is it?

## 48

The sun bakes them
The hand breaks them
The foot treads them
The mouth tastes them.

## 49

He's a boastful, puffed-up fellow,
Wearing spurs; eyes gleaming yellow.
As he proudly struts about
He's in charge, there is no doubt.

## 50

My first is in bottle but isn't in milk,
My second's in satin but isn't in silk,
My third and my fourth are both in
a pair,
My fifth is in hope and also despair,
My last is in yellow but isn't in
pink,
My whole contains liquid for people
to drink.

## 51

What is it that leaps and runs
And has no feet?

## 52

Two little holes
In the side of a hill
Just as you come
To the cherry-red mill.

## 53

What runs round the garden without
moving?

## 54

My first is in fish and also in chips,
My second's in mouth but not in
lips,
My third is in ache but not in pain,
My fourth is my third all over again,
My fifth is in pupil but isn't in class,
My whole is a beast that feeds on
the grass.

## 55

A father's child
A mother's child
Yet no one's son.

## 56

My voice is tender
My waist is slender
I'm often invited to play.
Yet wherever I go
I must take my bow
Or else I have nothing to say.

## 57

We are a pair,
We can dart here and there,
Though we always stay in one place.
We can smile or shed tears,
Show our pleasure or fears,
And you'll find us on everyone's
face.

## 58

White and thin,
Red within,
With a nail at the end.

## 59

I'm very tempting, so it's said,
I have a shiny coat of red,
And my flesh is white beneath.
I smell so sweet,
Taste good to eat,
And help to guard your teeth.

## 60

I daily am in France and Spain,
At times do all the world explore,
Since time began I've held my reign,
And shall till time will be no more.
I never in my life have strolled
In garden, field, or city park,
Yet all of these are sad and cold
If I'm not there and it is dark.

## 61

Without a bridle, or a saddle,
Across a thing I ride a-straddle.
And those I ride, by help of me,
Though almost blind, are made to
see.

## 62

I open wide and tight I shut,
Sharp am I and paper cut –
Fingers too, so do take care,
I'm good and bad, so best beware.

## 63

What has black spots and a white
face,
Is fat not thin, and helps you to
win,
But tumbles all over the place?

## 64

I have no voice and yet I speak to
you,
I tell of all things in the world that
people do;
I have leaves, but I am not a tree,
I have pages, but I am not a bride or
royalty;
I have a spine and hinges, but I am
not a man or a door,
I have told you all,
I cannot tell you more.

## 65

There is a thing that nothing is,
And yet it has a name:
It's sometimes tall
And sometimes short,
It tumbles if we fall.
It joins our sport,
And plays at every game.

## 66

More eyes have I than I do need for
sight,
A cry have I that is both sharp and
clear,
A tail have I more fit for show than
flight,
Admired am I wherever I appear.

## 67

I move silently without wings,
Between silvery, silken strings,
And there stretched in the grass
You'll see my web as you pass.

## 68

No mouth, no eyes,
Nor yet a nose,
Two arms, two feet,
And as it goes,
The feet don't touch the ground,
But all the way the head runs round.

## 69

My first is in dog but isn't in cat,
My second's in glove but not in hat,
My third is in flame but isn't in
smoke,
My fourth is in jester but not in
joke.
My whole makes no fuss about what
it will eat,
And is known to be nimble on its
four feet.

## 70

What is it
That has teeth
And can't eat?

## 71

Mother and father, sister and
brother,
All running after one another,
Each pair running behind the other,
Bet they'll never catch each other.

## 72

I'm a busy active creature,
Full of mirth and play by nature;
Nimbly I skip from tree to tree,
To get the food that's fit for me;
Then let me hear, if you can tell,
What is my name and where I
dwell.

## 73

From house to house I go,
Sometimes narrow, sometimes wide.
And whether there's rain or snow
I always stay outside.

## 74

A very pretty thing am I,
Fluttering in the pale-blue sky.
Delicate, fragile on the wing,
Indeed I am a pretty thing.

## 75

Two bodies have I
Though both joined in one.
The more still I stand
The quicker I run.

## 76

Little Nancy Etticoat
Has a white petticoat
And a red nose.
She has no feet or hands;
The longer she stands
The shorter she grows.

## 77

What flares up
And does a lot of good,
And when it dies,
It's just a piece of wood?

## 78

High in the sky
I can see with my eye
White horses are grazing.
Isn't that amazing?

## 79

What is full of holes and holds
water?

## 80

Old Mother Twitchett has but one
eye,
And a long tail which she can let
fly,
And every time she goes over a gap,
She leaves a bit of her tail in a trap.

## 81

As black as ink and is not ink,
As white as milk and is not milk,
As soft as silk and is not silk,
And is a thief but does not know it.

## 82

The beginning of eternity,
The end of time and space,
The beginning of every end,
And the end of every place.

## 83

Look in my face, I am somebody;
Look in my back, I am nobody.

## 84

Headed like a thimble,
Tailed like a rat.
You may guess to Doomsday,
But you couldn't guess that.

## 85

You would scarcely believe
That one dwarf could heave
A whole mountain range
On our lawn. That's strange!

## 86

What is it that has four legs
And one back,
Yet can't walk?

## 87

My first is in wood but isn't in tree,
My second's in four and also in
three,
My third is in music and also in
tune,
My fourth is in May but isn't in
June.
My whole makes a noise
You can hear down the street.
What am I?

## 88

First you see me in the grass
Dressed in yellow gay;
Next I am in dainty white,
Then I fly away.

## 89

In spring I am gay
In handsome array;
In summer more clothing I wear;
When colder it grows
I fling off my clothes;
And in winter quite naked appear.

## 90

Hands she has but does not hold,
Teeth she has but does not bite,
Feet she has but they are cold,
Eyes she has but without sight.
Who is she?

## 91

As I went over Lincoln Bridge,
I met Mister Rusticap;
Pins and needles on his back,
A-going to Thorny Fair.

## 92

Its headscarf is red,
And it grows in the ground.
When it shakes its bald head,
You can hear a loud sound.

## 93

To cross the water I'm the way,
For water I'm above:
I touch it not and, truth to say,
I neither swim nor move.

## 94

Black within,
Red without,
Four corners round about.

## 95

Violet, indigo, blue and green,
Yellow, orange and red,
These are the colours you have seen
After the storm has fled.

## 96

What is the thing which,
Once poured out,
Cannot be gathered again?

## 97

Round as an apple,
Deep as a cup,
All the King's horses
Can't pull it up.

## 98

What is it
That makes tears without sorrow
And takes its journey to heaven?

## 99

As long as I live I eat,
But when I drink I die.

## 100

What is it?
The more you take from it,
The larger it gets.

## 101

What always goes to bed with his
shoes on?

# Answers

*page 5*
riddle

| | | | |
|---|---|---|---|
| 1 cabbage | 6 moon | 26 egg | 30 walnut |
| 2 mouse | 7 fish | 27 cherry | 31 bee |
| 3 river | 8 rabbit | 28 orange | 32 duck |
| 4 bat | 9 owl | 29 blackberry | 33 ladybird |
| 5 bed | | | |

| | | | |
|---|---|---|---|
| 10 key | 14 dove | 34 sailing ship | 39 frog |
| 11 cat | 15 horse and rider | 35 crab | 40 water |
| 12 snowman | 16 windmill | 36 darkness | 41 snail |
| 13 icicle | | 37 star | 42 sea |
| | | 38 anchor | |

| | | | |
|---|---|---|---|
| 17 toadstool | 21 swallow | 43 onion | 47 broom |
| 18 kite | 22 footstep | 44 comb | 48 grapes |
| 19 bell | 23 cow | 45 pig | 49 cockerel |
| 20 lantern | 24 pair of shoes | 46 gloves | 50 barrel |
| | 25 saw | | |

# Answers

| | | | |
|---|---|---|---|
| 51 ball | 56 violin | 75 hourglass | 80 needle and thread |
| 52 nose and mouth | 57 eyes | 76 candle | 81 magpie |
| 53 fence | 58 finger | 77 match | 82 letter E |
| 54 sheep | 59 apple | 78 clouds | 83 mirror |
| 55 girl | | 79 sponge | 84 pipe |

| | | | |
|---|---|---|---|
| 60 sun | 64 book | 85 mole | 89 tree |
| 61 spectacles | 65 shadow | 86 chair | 90 doll |
| 62 scissors | 66 peacock | 87 drum | 91 hedgehog |
| 63 dice | | 88 dandelion | 92 poppy |

| | | | |
|---|---|---|---|
| 67 spider | 71 four wheels | 93 bridge | 97 well |
| 68 wheelbarrow | 72 squirrel | 94 chimney | 98 smoke |
| 69 goat | 73 path | 95 rainbow | 99 fire |
| 70 rake | 74 butterfly | 96 rain | 100 ditch |
| | | | 101 horse |